The
Circle
Maker

Participant's Guide

The Circle Maker

Participant's Guide

Four Sessions

Praying Circles Around Your
Biggest Dreams and Greatest Fears

Mark Batterson

with Kevin and Sherry Harney

ZONDERVAN.com/
AUTHORTRACKER
follow your favorite authors

ZONDERVAN

The Circle Maker Participant's Guide
Copyright © 2011 by Mark Batterson

This title is also available as a Zondervan ebook. Visit www.zondervan.com/ebooks.

Requests for information should be addressed to:
Zondervan, *Grand Rapids, Michigan 49530*

ISBN 978-0-310-33309-8

Published in association with the literary agency of Fedd & Company, Inc., Post Office Box 341973, Austin, TX 78734.

Cover design: *Extra Credit Projects*
Interior illustration: *istockphoto®*
Interior design: *Beth Shagene*

Printed in the United States of America

16 17 18 /DCI/ 21 20 19 18 17 16

Contents

A Word
from Mark Batterson

There is nothing God loves more than keeping promises, answering prayers, performing miracles, and fulfilling dreams. That is *who* He is. That is *what* He does.

The greatest moments in life are the miraculous moments when human impotence and divine omnipotence intersect — and this happens when we draw a circle of prayer around impossible situations in our lives and invite God to intervene.

It is absolutely imperative that followers of Jesus come to terms with this simple yet life-changing truth: *God is for us*. If we do not believe this, we will pray small and timid prayers. If we live with confidence that God is for us, we will pray big, audacious prayers.

Prayers are prophecies. They are the best predictors of our spiritual future. Who we become is determined by how we pray. Ultimately, the transcript of our prayers becomes the script of our lives.

In this four-session small group curriculum, you will learn how to claim God-given promises, pursue God-sized dreams, and seize God-ordained opportunities. You will learn how to draw prayer circles around your family, your job, your church, your problems, your goals, and your dreams.

As you discover the power of becoming a circle maker, it is essential that you understand this is not learning some magic trick or manipulative system to get what you want from God. The One who made the universe is not some genie in a bottle who pops out when we decide we need Him saying, "Your wish is my command." If we want to experience powerful prayer, His command needs to be our wish! If it is not, we won't be drawing prayer circles, but we will end up walking in circles.

In the coming weeks you will dig deep into God's Word, hear and tell many stories of faith, and learn about circle making. By God's grace and with the leading of the Holy Spirit, you will become a circle maker and enter a new season of joy, effectiveness, and power in prayer. You will learn that drawing prayer circles starts with discerning what God wants and wills. Until His sovereign will becomes your sanctified wish, your prayer life will be unplugged from its power supply. When you plug into God's will and power supply, you will learn to draw prayer circles around the promises, miracles, and dreams God wants for you.

Know that as you learn together as a group, I have circled you in prayer and I have a holy anticipation that God is going to do amazing things in and through you.

Enjoy the journey,
Mark Batterson

Of Note

The quotations interspersed throughout this participant's guide are excerpts from the book *The Circle Maker* by Mark Batterson and from the DVD curriculum of the same name. All other resources — including the small group questions, introductions, and between-sessions materials — have been written by Kevin and Sherry Harney in collaboration with Mark Batterson.

Session 1

Becoming
a Circle Maker

God loves to make promises. He invites us to draw a circle around those promises and pray until we see them become a reality. God is inviting you and me into the adventure of seeing His dreams come true in this world. This happens as we make the decision to become circle makers.

Introduction

People today love extreme sports!

We live in a world where the boundaries of human ability and capacity continue to be pressed and stretched. People compete in Ironman Triathlons where they swim 2.4 miles, bike 112 miles, and *then* run a full marathon of 26.2 miles.

Freestyle motorcycle riders used to dream of doing a backflip and landing it. Few dared even try it. That move is now commonplace ... riders are *expected* to do it. So, in 2006, a rider named Travis Pastrana attempted and landed a double backflip on a motorcycle in the X Games. No doubt, someone out there today is trying to figure out how they will land a triple backflip on a motorcycle.

Extreme sports like ice climbing, wingsuit base jumping, kayak skydiving, snocross, and a myriad of other surprising options are cropping up as people look for a new rush of adrenaline and a greater challenge.

Something in the human spirit pushes us to climb higher, drive faster, and push the boundaries. Into this world of risk-taking adventurers God whispers an invitation, "Try drawing a prayer circle!" Into the lives of Christians who have become bored with the same old religious practices and routine spiritual lives, the Spirit of God says, "Take a risk, draw a circle, and engage your faith at a whole new level." For believers who love God with a passion, but have slipped into a spiritual rut, it is time to enter a whole new level of extreme faith ... it is time to become a circle maker!

At the end of the day, and the end of your life, you will look back and discover that one of the most extreme things you could ever do is draw a circle.

The greatest moments in life are the miraculous moments when human impotence and divine omnipotence intersect — and they intersect when we draw a circle around the impossible situations in our lives and invite God to intervene.

Talk About It

Tell about a time you did something risky or extreme. What moved you to do something adventurous like this?

Who you become is determined by how you pray. Ultimately, the transcript of your prayers becomes the script of your life.

Video Teaching Notes

As you watch the video teaching segment for session one, use the following outline to record thoughts and reflections that stand out to you.

Drawing a prayer circle around Capitol Hill

The Legend of Honi the Circle Maker

The Jericho miracle

Identifying your Jericho

Wayne and Diane's circle makers' story

Know what to circle

Learning from Daniel: finding a time and place

The 21-day challenge

 Drawing prayer circles starts with discerning what God wants, what God wills. And until His sovereign will becomes your sanctified wish, your prayer life will be unplugged from its power supply.

Video Discussion

1. Mark shares his story of feeling under qualified and overwhelmed when he started National Community Church. Tell about a time you faced a real-life situation and you felt under qualified and overwhelmed.

When we feel under qualified and overwhelmed, we might be exactly where God wants us. These moments force us to pray like everything depends on God. They also drive us to our knees. In times like this we move to a place of raw dependence on God and raw dependence is the raw material out of which God performs His greatest miracles.

2. **Read:** Numbers 13:26 – 33. Describe the territory God called Joshua and the people of Israel to enter and take as their own. What was the nature of this task and why would prayer be such an essential part of accomplishing it?

3. Mark tells the story about prayer-walking a specific area of Washington D.C. He marked an area; he made a map; then he circled it in prayer.

Take a moment and draw a map or picture of an area, relationship, goal, or something else that you believe God wants you to circle in prayer. It could be as simple as the name of a person, or a drawing of your neighborhood or workplace.

Next, write down three or four prayers you can begin to pray around this territory.

-

-

-

-

You may want to share with your group the place, situation, or person you feel God drawing you to and invite them to join you in drawing this circle.

4. Describe a time you prayed about something and God did far more than you expected.

5. Write down a specific time in your life when you experienced great blessing, a spiritual breakthrough, a miracle, or the fulfillment of a dream. Then, reflect back on the persons who were praying for you. Write down their names ... create a prayer genealogy.

A blessing I experienced, breakthrough, miracle, or dream:

Names of persons who prayed:

Briefly share this story with your group, and then pause as a group to lift up a few focused prayers of thanks for these people who are in your spiritual genealogy and who circled you in prayer.

> *I believe that every blessing, every breakthrough, every miracle, and every dream has a genealogy. If you trace it all the way back to its origin, you will find a prayer circle.*

6. Why is it important that we have people in our lives who draw circles of prayer around us? Who is praying for you right now and how can you help them stay informed so that they can continue to pray in specific and powerful ways? This might be a great time to thank them in some tangible way.

7. Who are *you* praying for regularly and how are your prayers impacting the lives of these people? How can you increase the intensity of the prayer circles you are drawing for these people?

Miracles are the by-product of prayers that were prayed by you or for you. And that should be all the motivation you need to pray.

8. **Read:** James 4:1 – 3. Mark says in the video: "God has determined that certain expressions of His power will only be exercised in response to prayer. Simply put: We have not because we ask not. Put another way, we have not because we circle not."

How do you respond to this idea that some things don't happen because we choose not to pray and circle these things?

What might be an example of something we would miss because we make a choice not to pray?

What is something you have *not* been circling in prayer that you now feel you need to engage with a whole new level of seriousness? What steps will you take to circle this matter in prayer and how can your group members come alongside of you?

9. When Honi prayed, and then the rain began to fall ... he did not stop praying! He began to pray with greater specificity. First, he prayed for more rain ... rain that would fill cisterns, pits, and caverns. He asked God for an outpouring that people would remember for decades. Then, he prayed for a rain of God's favor, blessing, and grace. Wow! What boldness! Sometimes we pray small and unfocused prayers when God wants us to draw circles that are big and specific.

Think about the map you drew earlier in this session and the list of prayers you wrote down. Look at the map and read the prayers. Now, rewrite those prayers with two things in mind: (1) How can I be bolder and dare to ask even more? (2) How can I be more specific and detailed in how I circle this territory in prayer?

Next, rewrite some examples of how you can circle this person, need, thing, or situation in prayer. Be bold and precise!

•

•

•

•

Share your new prayer direction with your group members and invite them to pray with similar boldness and precision.

10. **Read:** Joshua 6:1 – 15. How do you think the people of Israel felt as they approached Jericho and saw the mammoth walls and extraordinary fortification of this fortress-city?

What is the Jericho in your life right now? You know God is powerful and you trust Him, but if the truth were known, there are moments when you wonder if this wall will ever fall, if you will ever see the victory of God in this specific area. Share your journey of facing this Jericho and how you feel about it today.

Jericho is spelled lots of different ways. If you have cancer, it's spelled healing. If your child is far from God, it's spelled salvation. If your marriage is falling apart, it's spelled reconciliation. If you have a vision that is beyond your resources, it's spelled provision.

11. **Read:** Matthew 20:29 – 34. If Jesus were to meet you face-to-face and ask, "What do You want me to do for you?" what would you answer? What would you dare to ask of Jesus ... and have the confidence that it is something He wants to accomplish in and through you?

Well-developed faith results in well-defined prayers, and well-defined prayers result in a well-lived life.

Closing Prayer

Take time as a group to pray in some of the following directions...

- Thank God for the people He has used in your life to circle you in prayer.

- Confess that there have been times when you missed out on opportunities to draw precise and bold prayer circles and pray that these moments would be less frequent.

- Lift up a need of one of your group members in prayer and circle them with confidence.

- Invite the Holy Spirit to prompt, convict, and move you to deeper places of prayer.

Bold prayers honor God, and God honors bold prayers. God isn't offended by your biggest dreams or boldest prayers. He is offended by anything less. If your prayers aren't impossible to you, they are insulting to God. Why? Because they don't require divine intervention.

Between Sessions

Personal Reflection

Take time in personal reflection and think about the following questions ...

- What is a specific situation I am facing that needs to be circled in prayer and what has kept me from praying with bold confidence?

- How has God been faithful to answer prayers in my past and how can my awareness of God's work in the past give me confidence for the future?

- What is my next step in growing as a circle maker?

- Who do I know who needs to learn to draw bold circles of prayer and how can I tell that person about what I have been learning about prayer?

Personal Actions

21-Day Prayer Challenge

Try a prayer challenge starting today, and for the next twenty-one days. Using the space provided on page 28, identify a time you will pray every day. Then, pick a place you will go consistently to meet with God in prayer. Be sure this is a place you feel connected to God. Finally, identify a specific person, promise, or problem you will circle in prayer every day for the coming three weeks. Be sure to keep this appointment with God every day and see what He accomplishes in and through you.

My Prayer *Time*:

My Prayer *Place*:

The *Person*, *Promise*, or *Problem* I will circle:

Results from my prayer circling challenge:

Prayer Walk

If you have never prayer-walked before, use the simple directions below to help get you started:

1. Identify a specific location you know God wants you to pray for. You might even want to draw a picture of this place. It could be a home, workplace, school, community building, a block, or even a neighborhood.

2. Make a short list of three or four things you believe God wants you to pray while you walk around this area. It could be needs

for specific people, salvation for those who are far from God, an in-breaking of God's Holy Spirit, conviction of sin, safety, the breaking of spiritual strongholds, or anything else God places on your heart.

3. Plan to do your walk (on your own or with others you might invite along). Then go out and do it. You can pray silently or out loud. If you are with another person or a group and you pray out loud, others will think you are having a conversation with each other. If you are alone, if you pray in a normal and conversational tone, people will think you are talking on a Bluetooth or phone!

4. Keep praying for these same needs and concerns after you have completed your prayer circle walk.

> *Not every prayer will be answered the way we script it, but I'm convinced of this: The miracles that have happened would not have happened if I hadn't drawn a circle around them in the first place.*

Recommended Reading

As you reflect on what you have learned in this session, you may want to read the opening section of the book, *The Circle Maker*, by Mark Batterson, chapters 1 – 4. In preparation for session two you might want to read the section, The First Circle, chapters 5 – 7.

> *Don't just read the Bible. Start circling the promises. Don't just make a wish. Write down a list of God-glorifying life goals. Don't just pray. Keep a journal.*

JOURNAL, REFLECTIONS, AND NOTES

Session 2

Little People, Big Risks, and Huge Circles

Can the dreams and prayers of one person really make a difference? Absolutely!

God is bigger and more powerful than we imagine. When our dreams grow as big as the heart and power of God, we begin experiencing answers to prayers that can be defined as nothing less than miraculous.

Introduction

Have you ever thought about how many times a little occurrence has surprisingly BIG consequences? Drop a pebble into a still pond and watch the ripples work their way outward in concentric circles that seem to go on and on. Speak a sentence of gossip to one or two people and watch the shock waves of poison spread through a family, church, or community as those "private" and "secret" words are passed on from one person to another until everyone knows. Sometimes a small or seemingly inconsequential action has enormous repercussions.

Think about a shift in the crust of the earth along a fault line. This small movement of inches or feet can send shock waves of movement for miles and redefine an entire landscape.

In a very similar way, God loves to take small, ordinary, and surprising people and accomplish huge things for His glory. All through the Bible, and all through history, God has sent ripples of His glory and power through the world as people like you and me have learned that their dreams and prayers can grow as big as the God they love.

Never underestimate the power of a single prayer. God can do anything through anyone who circles their big dreams with bold prayers. With God, there is no precedent, because all things are possible.

Talk About It

Mark talks about going to the roof of Ebenezer's Coffeehouse, the National Cathedral, or the Lincoln Memorial when he wants to dream big and pray hard. Where do you go when you want to get face-to-face with God and seek to dream big dreams for Him? Why is this place special to you and how does it connect you to God and His power?

If you keep praying, you'll keep dreaming, and conversely, if you keep dreaming, you'll keep praying. Dreaming is a form of praying, and praying is a form of dreaming. The more you pray, the bigger your dreams will become.

Video Teaching Notes

As you watch the video teaching segment for session two, use the following outline to record thoughts and reflections that stand out to you.

One woman; one vision; one prayer

The bigness of God

What defines a big dream?

Risk-taking: being willing to look foolish

Dare to dream big and pray hard

Cloudy with a chance of quail: Numbers 13

The important question

Renee's circle maker's story

 One litmus test of spiritual maturity is whether your dreams are getting bigger or smaller.

Video Discussion

1. Tell about a time when you or someone else lifted up a big prayer and God's timing or answer was surprising.

2. Mark defines a "big dream" as something that is bigger than you and beyond your human ability to accomplish. Take a moment to write down two or three dreams you have that you feel would honor God, and are clearly beyond your ability to accomplish on your own. They could be dreams for your life, family, church, community, or anything God places on your heart.

   •

   •

   •

   Tell your small group about one of these dreams and ask them to join you in praying that God would accomplish this dream in and through your life, if this is His desire.

 You are only one defining decision away from a totally different life. One defining decision can change your trajectory and put you on a new path toward the Promised Land.

3. In the Legend of the Circle Maker, Honi drew himself into a prayer circle and took a huge risk. He said he would not leave the circle until it rained. To the outside observer, there is a fine line between faith and foolishness. What is this difference? How can fear of looking foolish keep us from taking risks for God?

4. The Bible is filled with examples of people who risked looking foolish for the sake of following God's plan for their lives. Noah built a huge ark in a desert; the Israelite army marched around Jericho blowing trumpets; David the shepherd boy faced a giant in battle with only a sling and a pocket full of rocks; Peter got out of a boat in the middle of a storm; and the list goes on.

    What are some ways God calls His children today to take risks that could make them look foolish? What happens when we risk looking foolish for the sake of God? What might we miss if we play it safe and never take a chance for God because we don't want to look foolish?

5. Mark makes this statement: "Moses learned this lesson well ... if you don't take the risk, you forfeit the miracle."

Tell about a time you took a risk for God and could have looked foolish, but God showed up and did something you could have never done on your own.

or

Tell about a time you did not dare to take a risk. What did you miss out on because you were not willing to look foolish and trust God enough to show up and accomplish what you could not?

6. Mark tells how God went ahead of him to prepare a place for National Community Church to meet in Union Station. God had actually been setting the table almost nine decades earlier

through President Teddy Roosevelt. God had orchestrated a movement in the AMC Theaters' national business plan that would open doors for the church. Mark knew none of this when he prayed circles around Union Station and finally walked in to talk with the theater manager. Tell about a time you prayed passionately, took a risk for God, and discovered that He had already gone ahead of you and prepared the way.

7. **Read:** Revelation 3:7. God opens doors and He closes them. Tell about a time God closed a door in your life, but later opened a better one. How did you feel when the door was first closed? How did your outlook change when God opened another door and you realized why He had closed a door earlier?

I think God is sometimes amazed at how small our plans are. He allows our small plans to fail so that His big dream for us can prevail.

8. **Read:** Numbers 11:4 – 23, 31 – 32. How was God's answer to Moses' prayer above and beyond what he could have imagined? How has God answered your prayers and treated you in ways that were beyond your wildest dreams?

9. Mark makes the statement, "Sometimes we reduce God to the size of our worst failure or greatest fear." How have you seen someone (including yourself) do this? What is the danger of limiting God to what we have experienced?

10. If our biggest problem is a small view of God, we need to expand our understanding of Him and let our dreams grow larger and larger! God-sized dreams can seem impossible, foolish, and shocking. Take time as a group to dream and pray about your church. *(cont.)*

What are three or four God-sized dreams God might want to accomplish in and through your church?

-

-

-

-

What is standing in the way of these dreams becoming a reality?

Who is praying regularly, passionately, and faithfully for dreams like this to become a reality in and through the life of your congregation?

What steps can your group take to lead the way in seeing these dreams come true?

 The size of prayers depends on the size of our God. And if God knows no limits, then neither should our prayers.

Closing Prayer

Take time as a group to pray in some of the following directions ...

- Ask God to give you courage to risk foolishness for the sake of praying big prayers and drawing big circles.

- Thank God for His greatness and ask for hearts and minds that grow more aware of His glorious vastness and sovereign omnipotence.

- Pray for your church to dream as big as the God you worship.

- Lift up specific prayers for your local church and ask God for provision that is so plentiful that only God could bring it and only He can receive the glory!

Prayer is the alpha and omega of planning. Don't just brainstorm; praystorm.

Between Sessions

Personal Reflection

We live in a culture where people are terrified of looking foolish. We have become pathologically concerned about what everyone else thinks about us. It is time to risk foolishness for the sake of what God desires to do in and through us ... for His glory.

Make time in the coming days to get away somewhere quiet and reflect on any of the following questions:

- When was the last time I risked looking foolish for the sake of Jesus ... the one who faced mocking, public disgrace, and crucifixion for me?

- What keeps me from taking genuine risks for God?

- What are the moments when God invites me to risk looking foolish, but I tend to guard my reputation and appearance in the eyes of others?

- How will I respond differently the next time I face one of these opportunities to take a risk for God?

- How can I begin praying for God to work in and through me, even when I am fearful of looking foolish?

Personal Action

Read: Matthew 14:22 – 32. Mark gives a simple and wise challenge at the end of this video session: like Peter, we need to get out of the boat if we want to experience walking on water. But he also warns,

"If Jesus has *not* said come, you had better stay in the boat and not try to walk on the water."

Take time to reflect on your life and identify an area of life in which you know Jesus is calling you to get out of the boat and walk toward Him. This should not be a personal idea that Jesus is *not* behind, but one He has been forming in your heart, bringing to your mind, and speaking to you about over and over.

Make a decision to draw a prayer circle around this big, Jesus-led dream. Then, get a few close friends praying with and for you. Finally, take the first step out of the boat and see what God does!

Sometimes the power of prayer is the power to carry on. It doesn't always change your circumstances, but it gives you the strength to walk through them.

Recommended Reading

As you reflect on what you have learned in this session, you may want to reread the section, The First Circle, chapters 5 – 7 in the book, *The Circle Maker*, by Mark Batterson. In preparation for session three you might want to read the section, The Second Circle, chapters 8 – 11.

May you keep dreaming until the day you die.
May imagination overtake memory.
May you die young at a ripe old age.

JOURNAL, REFLECTIONS, AND NOTES

Praying Hard and Praying Through

Too many people grow weary and quit praying. If we want to see God's miracles come true in our lives, church, and world, we need to persist in prayer, even when we grow tired, feel foolish, and think the situation is hopeless. We need to pray hard and pray through!

Introduction

A family from Iowa embarks on a long-awaited road trip to the West Coast to see the Pacific Ocean. Traveling across Nebraska, Colorado, Utah, and Nevada, they finally reach California. Their anticipation of ocean vistas and rugged coastlines surges. After several more hours of driving they see a sign: MONTEREY WHARF, 2 MILES. Then, for no apparent reason, Dad makes a U-turn and begins to head back to Iowa. He mutters to Mom and the kids, "I think we've seen enough. Let's head home."

It is Friday night, the lights are hot, and everyone in town is at the high school football game. With time running out, the home team running back receives the ball on the fifteen-yard line, eighty-five yards from a touchdown and come-from-behind victory. Breaking through the line of scrimmage, he sees nothing but open field in front of him and sprints for the end zone. But five yards from the goal line he stops and sits down.

These are two scenarios you will probably never see. When you drive across the country to see the Pacific Ocean and get a couple of miles from it, you finish the trip so you can stand in stunned wonder at the pounding of the waves along the rugged coast. When a running back breaks clear of the defense and sees the end zone two or three strides away, he races in and revels in the victory! Anything less would seem absurd.

Yet, as strange as these two scenarios seem, something far more shocking happens every day. People quit praying. They have prayed hard for months or years, and then they just stop. They grow weary, discouraged, or they simply get distracted. For all they know they are two miles from the coast or five yards from the end zone. Too often prayer is abandoned before the goal is met ... and sometimes this happens when God's answer is just around the bend.

The results of our prayers are far more important than seeing the coast or scoring a touchdown. Our prayers can have eternal consequences. We need to learn to persist in prayer and press through all the way to the end.

> *The reason many of us give up too soon is that we feel like we have failed if God doesn't answer our prayer. That isn't failure. The only way you can fail is if you stop praying.*

Talk About It

Share about a time when you worked hard at something but then gave up before you completed it or crossed the finish line. As you look back on that moment, what runs through your mind?

or

Share about a time when you worked hard at something, and though you wanted to quit, you completed the task and reached your desired goal. How did that make you feel?

> *The circle maker's mantra: 100 percent of the prayers I don't pray won't get answered.*

Video Teaching Notes

As you watch the video teaching segment for session three, use the following outline to record thoughts and reflections that stand out to you.

From crack house to coffeehouse

The difference between praying for and praying hard

Elijah's standard of praying hard

Concrete steps of faith

Physical and spiritual contracts

Heidi's circle maker's story

Counterfactual theory

Praying hard is hard

Praying hard is more than words; it's blood, sweat, and tears. Praying hard is two-dimensional: praying like it depends on God, and working like it depends on you. It's praying until God answers, no matter how long it takes. It's doing whatever it takes to show God you're serious.

Video Discussion

1. Mark tells the story of circling an abandoned crack house in prayer for five years and then praying for another three years for the zoning and resources to build Ebenezer's Coffeehouse. It took almost a decade to move from a dream to a reality. Share about a time that you persisted in prayer for months or years and finally saw the prayer answered.

2. What is one need, concern, or dream that you have been circling in prayer for a long time, but the answer has still not come? What kind of discouragement or temptation to quit praying have you faced along the way? How have you resisted the temptation to quit praying?

3. Mother Dabney made God a promise. She prayed, "If You will bless my husband in the place You sent him to establish Your Name, if You break the bonds and destroy the middle wall of partition, if You will give him a church and a congregation — a credit to Your people and all Christendom — I will walk with You for three years in prayer — both day and night." What are the specific and focused prayers this godly woman lifted up? What do you think about her prayer and promise?

Prayer is a habit to be cultivated. It is a discipline to be developed. It is a skill to be practiced.

4. Mark suggests that "praying through" is all about intensity and consistency. What does it look like when we pray with intensity? Why is consistency important in prayer? What helps us grow in both intensity and consistency as we circle things in prayer?

Do you have a favorite place to pray where you feel a greater connection to God and your mind is more focused? What is it about this place that helps you pray and how can you make more time to get to this place?

5. **Read:** 1 Kings 18:41 – 46 and James 5:17 – 18. How is Elijah an example of persisting in prayer and expecting an answer from God? How can his example influence the way you pray and seek the face of God?

6. In session one of this study you drew a picture of a need, place, concern, or person and drew a prayer circle around it. Take a moment and look back at what you drew and circled. In the space provided on the next page, write two things. First, what would it look like if you committed to pray hard and pray through as you continue to circle this in prayer? Second, what actions can you take to partner with God as you continue praying for this specific thing?

How can I pray hard and pray through for what I circled in session one?

-

-

-

Actions I can take to partner with God:

-

-

-

Share one or more reflections and action goals with your group members and invite them to pray for you and keep you accountable to take action as you partner with God.

 Praying hard is standing on the promises of God. And when we stand on His word, God stands by His word. His word is His bond.

7. Mark points out that Elijah connected actions with his prayers. He prayed against the prophets of Baal *and* challenged them to a showdown. Elijah called the widow to bake a loaf of bread. And, he did more than pray for God to part the water of the Jordan ... he struck it with his cloak. Elijah took concrete steps of faith. What are some specific steps of faith you know God wants you to take as you are praying for the needs and challenges you face in your life?

8. Mark tells a wonderful story about going out and buying a drum set before the church had a drummer. What did you learn from this story? What is one step of faith you can take right now that would be a preemptive action showing that you trust God is ready to work on your behalf? (In other words, what is the drum set you need to buy?)

The reason God doesn't answer our prayers isn't that we aren't praying hard enough; the reason, more often than not, is that we aren't willing to work hard enough. Praying hard is synonymous with working hard.

9. A. W. Tozer said, "What comes to you when you think about God is the most important thing about you." On the video Mark expands on this idea and talks about two big images that come to his mind when he thinks about Jesus. What pictures come to your mind when you think of Jesus and what does this reveal about your view of Him as God? How can your vision of God impact the way you pray and the bigness of the requests you make?

10. Counterfactual theory explores what might have happened in history if things had ended differently. Mark suggests that things could have been very different if the Israelites had stopped circling Jericho after six days and failed to press on the seventh day ... the wall would not have fallen. In a similar way, if Elijah had not prayed the seventh time but quit after six times, the rain would not have come. Do you believe our prayers, faith, and willingness to follow God really make that much of an impact? If so, give an example.

11. Respond to this statement: "We give up too easily. We give up too soon. Sometimes we quit praying right before the miracle happens."

How can your group members encourage and inspire each other to keep praying, even when it gets hard? How can you keep each other accountable to add actions to your prayers as you partner with God?

When you pray through, the burden is taken off of your shoulders and put on the shoulders of Him who carried the cross of Calvary.

Closing Prayer

Take time as a group to pray in some of the following directions . . .

- Thank God for being patient and gracious even when we give in, give up, and stop praying.

- Ask for power to pray hard and pray through . . . even when you feel weary and discouraged.

- Confess when you have given up and quit praying and ask for courage and devotion to start praying again.

- Lift up one of your group members and ask God to help him or her pray hard and keep praying, even though the journey has been long and tiring. Pray for a fresh filling of the Spirit in your group member's heart and for renewed courage.

 Part of praying hard is persisting in prayer even when we don't get the answer we want. It's choosing to believe that God has a better plan. And He always does!

Between Sessions

Personal Reflection

Take time in personal reflection to think about the following questions ...

- What are some of the prayers I have never dared to ask? What has kept me from asking them? How can I begin lifting up these prayers today?

- What are examples of times I have prayed hard, but failed to take action and do my part? What is an action I need to take to bring my life in alignment with my prayers?

Personal Action

We can't just pray like Elijah; we need to act like him. This means we need to take concrete actions as we pray. Write down three important prayer circles you are drawing right now. Then, write down two or three actions you could take as you pray for each. In the coming week, act on at least one of these possible actions:

Something I am circling in prayer:

Possible action I could take as I pray for this:

Possible action I could take as I pray for this:

Possible action I could take as I pray for this:

Something I am circling in prayer:

Possible action I could take as I pray for this:

Possible action I could take as I pray for this:

Possible action I could take as I pray for this:

Something I am circling in prayer:

Possible action I could take as I pray for this:

Possible action I could take as I pray for this:

Possible action I could take as I pray for this:

God is great not just because nothing is too big for Him;
God is great because nothing is too small for Him.

Recommended Reading

As you reflect on what you have learned in this session, you may want to reread the section, The Second Circle, chapters 8 – 11, in the book, *The Circle Maker*, by Mark Batterson. In preparation for session four you might want to read the sections, The Third Circle, chapters 12 – 15, and Keep Circling, chapters 16 – Afterword.

Some of the hardest moments in life are when you've prayed hard but the answer is "No" and you don't know why. And, you may never know why.
But that is the litmus test of trust.

JOURNAL, REFLECTIONS, AND NOTES

Session 4

Praying
Is Like Planting

We live in a time when all the data in the world is available with the click of a mouse. Into our fast-paced culture God speaks and reminds us that prayer is a lot like planting. It demands patience, consistency, and dependence on the only One who can bring rain.

Introduction

Picture a grandmother standing in the kitchen watching her grandson toss a bag of popcorn into the microwave and hit the popcorn button. She marvels as he fidgets impatiently, waiting "forever" for his snack to be ready. So, she sits him down for a chat as he munches on his popcorn and she tells him about how things used to be.

"You know, honey, when we wanted some popcorn when I was a little girl we had to take a pot out of the cabinet, pour some oil into it, and put it on the stove and wait as the oil heated up. Then, we would pour some popcorn kernels into the hot oil, put a lid on the pot, and jiggle and shake the pot until we heard the first pop. Then, we would shake the pot even harder as the rest of the kernels popped so they would not burn. Next, we would pour the popcorn into a big bowl. If we wanted butter on our popcorn — and I always did — we melted it in another pan on the stove and poured it over the popcorn. Finally, we would put on as much salt as we liked and we were ready to snack. Oh, and we had to clean up all the dishes when we were done and then put them away. But, it was so delicious ... and fun!"

The grandmother looks into her grandson's glazed eyes and realizes she might have given more of the history of popcorn than he wanted to hear, but she still dares to ask him, "Would you like to make some popcorn the old-fashioned way?"

He thinks for a moment and says, "That sounds like it would take all day. It takes long enough in the microwave," and he wanders from the room.

We live in a world where virtually everything comes quickly ... or we want it to. But prayer is like planting and then waiting for the harvest time. God does not promise instant results at the speed of light or even the speed of a microwave. Many prayers stay buried, growing slowly in the fertile soil of God's heart. But they *are* growing and they *will* bring a harvest. We just need to remain patient and keep praying!

> *Each prayer is like a seed that gets planted in the ground. It disappears for a season, but it eventually bears fruit that blesses future generations. In fact, our prayers bear fruit forever.*

Talk About It

Tell about a life experience where you had to wait patiently, much longer than you wanted to wait. How did this shape and form you? How might the experience have ended differently if you could have rushed things and made them happen quickly?

> *To dream big and pray hard, we need the patience of the planter. We need the foresight of the farmer. We need the mind-set of the sower.*

Video Teaching Notes

As you watch the video teaching segment for session four, use the following outline to record thoughts and reflections that stand out to you.

Time capsule prayers

Praying is like planting

Proximity and posture

David's 21-day breakthrough

Fasting as one form of circling

Michael's circle maker's story

All it takes is one person

White chalk circling

It takes time to discover the rhythms and routines that work for you. What works for others might not work for you, and what works for you might not work for others. I've always subscribed to a sentiment shared by Oswald Chambers: "Let God be as original with other people as He is with you."

Video Discussion

1. Mark tells the story about how he realized that God was preparing a new site for National Community Church all the way back in 1799 when Thomas Jefferson commissioned the Navy Yard. There followed in 1960 the prayers of evangelist R. W. Schambach and later those of Pastor Michael Hall. All of this happened by the leading of the Spirit and the direction of God's sovereign hand long before Mark or anyone else knew the seventh site for National Community Church.

   Look back through your life and identify some places where God was working long before you began praying and before a dream was ever ignited in your heart. Share one instance with your group.

We want things to happen at the speed of light instead of the speed of a seed planted in the ground.

2. Honi the Circle Maker met a man who was planting a tree that would not bear fruit for seventy years. The man explained that his father and grandfather had planted trees in their generations and that he was eating the fruit of those trees. We all have people in our lives who went before us and prayed, served, and planted trees of God's blessings that we are eating from today. Consider one person who came before you and had the

foresight to plant trees so that you could one day eat their fruit. How has the life of this person impacted you? What can you learn from his or her example?

3. As a church, it is important to look back and recognize the people who have served and prayed in ways that prepared the way for what we are experiencing today. Talk about some of the faithful saints in your church who have served, sacrificed, prayed, and believed God would do great things for His glory. What are some ways you can:

Remember these people:

Honor them:

Bless them (if they are still living):

Emulate their examples of faith:

Prayer is the inheritance we receive and the legacy we leave.

4. Mark recalls his grandfather kneeling at his bedside and praying over him with passion and consistency. Who is a person who did this for you and how are his or her prayers being answered? Who can you pray for in the same way and how might God use your prayers in the years to come?

5. **Read:** Daniel 6:1 – 10. What are some of the ways that life, and even our culture, can get in the way of us praying and devoting the time and passion we need to this important ministry? What can we do to notice and get around these roadblocks to prayer?

6. Daniel faced Jerusalem so he could be pointed in the direction of his dream as he prayed. He got himself in proximity because it helped him pray (not because it made the prayers more powerful). What are ways we can get in closer proximity to our dreams so we can pray with greater passion and focus?

Daniel's physical posture was a mirror of his mental and spiritual posture. What are some ways we can posture our bodies as we pray (use biblical examples) that will help us stay focused and concentrated on what we are drawing prayer circles around?

Drawing prayer circles is nothing more than laying our requests before God and waiting expectantly. If walking in circles helps you pray with more consistency and intensity, then make yourself dizzy; if not, then find something, find anything, that helps you pray through.

7. Mark reminds us that sometimes we need to just stop, drop, and pray. What is happening in your life right now that demands such immediate prayer attention, but your schedule and responsibilities have gotten in the way? How can your group members pray for and with you right now about this need, challenge, or situation?

It doesn't matter who you are or what you do. If you stop, drop, and pray, then you never know where you'll go, what you'll do, or who you'll meet.

8. **Read:** Daniel 10:1 – 21 and Ephesians 6:10 – 13. What do you learn about the reality of spiritual warfare and the battles we face as followers of Jesus? Why is it important that we recognize spiritual conflicts and are willing to enter into the battle in prayer?

9. What is the place of fasting, partnered with prayer, as we battle against the work of the enemy in this world? Tell about a time you fasted in partnership with prayer and the results of this pairing of two essential spiritual disciplines.

There is more than one way to draw a prayer circle. In fact, sometimes it involves more than prayer. I believe that fasting is a form of circling. In fact, an empty stomach may be the most powerful prayer posture in Scripture.

10. Daniel knew that his prayer and fasting would lead to a miracle of God that would happen long after he was dead. He pressed on knowing that the seeds he was planting would bear fruit for another generation. What are ways you can pray, fast, serve, and give (as an individual and small group) that will bear fruit for future generations in your local church?

11. **Read:** Matthew 7:7 – 8. What does Jesus call us to do in this passage and what does He promise? What is one specific and practical way you can follow this teaching and take action in the coming week? How can your group members pray with you and cheer you on as you move forward in this area of your life and faith?

Just as our greatest successes often come on the heels of our greatest failures, our greatest answers often come on the heels of our longest and most boring prayers. But, if you pray long and boring prayers, your life will be anything but boring. Your life will turn into the spiritual adventure it was destined to be. It won't always get you where you want to go, but it will get you through.

Closing Prayer

Take time as a group to pray in some of the following directions ...

- Ask God to help you stay patient in prayer so you can keep circling and planting for the sake of generations that will come after you. Pray for your children and grandchildren, nieces and nephews, and the coming generations ... even ones who are not yet born!

- Pray for your group members to have the courage, focus, and self-discipline to add fasting to their prayers as a regular part of their personal spiritual disciplines.

- Thank God for those people who planted seeds of prayer and circled your life in prayer long before you were aware they were doing it.

- Pray with anticipation for the time capsules of prayer others have buried for you and your church. They have not yet been opened, but they will be. Rejoice in what is yet to come.

- Ask God to give you direction about how the lessons in this study can influence and impact your local church and other congregations in your community.

Prayer is the way we escape the gravitational pull of the flesh and enter God's orbit. It's the way we escape our atmosphere and enter His space. It's the way we overcome our human limitations and enter the extradimensional realm where all things are possible.

In the Coming Weeks

Personal Reflection

Take time in the coming weeks to reflect on these questions ...

- What derails me from praying the way I should? What can I do to get past these hindrances and pray with greater power?

- How can I get in closer proximity to the things and people I need to pray for?

- What new prayer posture can I take to help me focus and become more intent in prayer?

- Who has prayed for me with faithful passion and how can I bless, honor, and affirm these people?

- When can I plan a time to pray and fast over something important?

Personal Actions

Since we are coming to a close of this study, here are three action ideas you can try in the coming weeks:

A 10-Day or 21-Day Time of Prayer and Fasting

Read: Daniel 6, 9 – 10. Then, plan a Daniel fast (fruits, vegetables, and water). You might want to make it for ten days or twenty-one days. Have a list of specific needs you will circle every day in a regular time of intercession. Also, pray for these needs every time your stomach cries out for food. Let your hunger for food drive you to hunger for God and pray with a voracious passion.

Try a New Posture

Scripture prescribes a wide variety of prayer postures such as kneeling (Psalm 95:6 – 7), falling prostrate on one's face (Nehemiah 8:5 – 6), standing (Nehemiah 8:5 – 6), lifting one's hands (Nehemiah 8:5 – 6; Psalm 141:2), laying on of hands (Luke 4:40), and anointing with oil (James 5:13 – 15). Physical postures help posture our hearts and minds. Try a new posture of prayer and see if this helps you focus on God with greater intensity.

> *There is nothing magical about the laying on of hands or bowing the knee or anointing the head with oil, but there is something biblical about it.*

Praying Through Your Calendar

Take time to pray through your calendar instead of just looking through it. It's amazing what a difference it makes when you pray circles around the people you will be meeting. It turns appointments into divine appointments. When you go into a meeting with a prayerful posture, it creates a positively charged atmosphere. Make a point of praying through the new week before you live it. Circle many things in prayer — people, meetings, tough settings you will encounter, tests, projects that are due, other deadlines, anything the Holy Spirit stirs in your heart.

> *What if we stopped reading the news and started praying it? What if lunch meetings turned into prayer meetings? What if we converted every problem, every opportunity, into a prayer? Maybe we'd come a lot closer to our goal of praying without ceasing.*

Recommended Reading

As you reflect on what you have learned in this session, you may want to reread the section, The Third Circle, chapters 12 – 15, and also the final section, Keep Circling, chapters 16 – Afterword.

 God answers every prayer, and He keeps every promise. That is who He is. That is what He does. And if you have the faith to dream big, pray hard, and think long, there is nothing God loves more than proving His faithfulness.

JOURNAL, REFLECTIONS, AND NOTES

Small Group
Leader Helps

To ensure a successful small group experience, read the following information before beginning.

Group Preparation

Whether your small group has been meeting together for years or is gathering for the first time, be sure to designate a consistent time and place to work through the four sessions. Once you establish the when and where of your times together, select a facilitator who will keep discussions on track and an eye on the clock. If you choose to rotate this responsibility, assign the four sessions to their respective facilitators up front, so that group members can prepare their thoughts and questions prior to the session they are responsible for leading. Follow the same assignment procedure should your group want to serve any snacks or beverages.

A Note to Facilitators

As facilitator, you are responsible for honoring the agreed-upon time frame of each meeting, for prompting helpful discussion among your group, and for keeping the dialogue equitable by drawing out quieter members and helping more talkative members to remember that others' insights are valued in your group.

You might find it helpful to preview each session's video teaching segment and then scan the "Video Discussion" questions that pertain to it, highlighting various questions that you want to be sure to cover during your group's meeting. Ask God in advance of your time together to guide your group's discussion, and then be sensitive to the direction He wishes to lead.

Urge participants to bring their participant's guide, pen, and a Bible to every gathering. Encourage them to consider buying a copy of *The Circle Maker* book by Mark Batterson to supplement this study.

Session Format

Each session of the participant's guide includes the following group components:

- **"Introduction"** — an entrée to the session's topic, which may be read by a volunteer or summarized by the facilitator

- **"Talk About It"** — an icebreaker question that relates to the session topic and invites input from every group member

- **"Video Teaching Notes"** — an outline of the session's video teaching (about 18 minutes each) for group members to follow along and take notes if they wish

- **"Video Discussion"** — video-related and Bible exploration questions that reinforce the session content and elicit personal input from every group member

- **"Closing Prayer"** — several prayer cues to guide group members in closing prayer

Additionally, in each session you will find a **"Between Sessions"** section that includes suggestions for personal response, recommended reading from *The Circle Maker* book, and two pages for journaling, reflections, or notes.

The Circle Maker

Praying Circles Around Your Biggest Dreams and Greatest Fears

Mark Batterson

According to Pastor Mark Batterson in his book, *The Circle Maker*, "Drawing prayer circles around our dreams isn't just a mechanism whereby we accomplish great things for God. It's a mechanism whereby God accomplishes great things in us."

Do you ever sense that there's far more to prayer, and to God's vision for your life, than what you're experiencing? It's time you learned from the legend of Honi the Circle Maker—a man bold enough to draw a circle in the sand and not budge from inside it until God answered his prayers for his people.

What impossibly big dream is God calling you to draw a prayer circle around? Sharing inspiring stories from his own experiences as a circle maker, Mark Batterson will help you uncover your heart's deepest desires and God-given dreams and unleash them through the kind of audacious prayer that God delights to answer.

Available in stores and online!

Share Your Thoughts

With the Author: Your comments will be forwarded to the author when you send them to *zauthor@zondervan.com*.

With Zondervan: Submit your review of this book by writing to *zreview@zondervan.com*.

Free Online Resources at
www.zondervan.com

Zondervan AuthorTracker: Be notified whenever your favorite authors publish new books, go on tour, or post an update about what's happening in their lives at www.zondervan.com/ authortracker.

Daily Bible Verses and Devotions: Enrich your life with daily Bible verses or devotions that help you start every morning focused on God. Visit www.zondervan.com/newsletters.

Free Email Publications: Sign up for newsletters on Christian living, academic resources, church ministry, fiction, children's resources, and more. Visit www.zondervan.com/newsletters.

Zondervan Bible Search: Find and compare Bible passages in a variety of translations at www.zondervanbiblesearch.com.

Other Benefits: Register to receive online benefits like coupons and special offers, or to participate in research.

ZONDERVAN.com/
AUTHORTRACKER
follow your favorite authors